D1029880

THE ADVENTURES OF MEDICAL MAN

Kids' Illnesses and Injuries Explained

Nut Allergy • Concussion • Broken Bones
Strep Throat • Ear Infection • Asthma

By Michael Evans, M.D., and David Wichman
Art by Gareth Williams

annick press
toronto + new york + vancouver

We acknowledge the support of the Canada Council for the Arts, the Ontario Arts Council, and the Government of Canada through the Canada Book Fund (CBF) for our publishing activities.

ONTARIO ARTS COUNCIL
CONSEIL DES ARTS DE L'ONTARIO

Cataloging in Publication

Evans, Michael, 1964-
    The adventures of Medical Man : kids' illnesses and injuries explained / by Michael Evans and David Wichman ; art by Gareth Williams.

Includes index.
ISBN 978-1-55451-263-8 (bound).—ISBN 978-1-55451-262-1 (pbk.)

    1. Diseases—Juvenile literature.   2. Wounds and injuries—Juvenile literature.
3. Medicine—Juvenile literature.   I. Wichman, David   II. Williams, Gareth Glyn
III. Title.

R130.5.E83 2010   j610   C2010-903124-5

Distributed in Canada by:
Firefly Books Ltd.
66 Leek Crescent
Richmond Hill, ON
L4B 1H1

Published in the U.S.A. by:
Annick Press (U.S.) Ltd.
Distributed in the U.S.A. by:
Firefly Books (U.S.) Inc.
P.O. Box 1338
Ellicott Station
Buffalo, NY 14205

Printed in China.

Visit us at: www.annickpress.com

For my four real heroes: Willa, Finn, Angus, and Sue
—M.E.

For my medical superheroes:
Dr. Jonathan Irish and Dr. Brian O'Sullivan
—D.W.

CONTENTS

INTRODUCTION

Hi, I'm Dr. Michael Evans. I'm not a movie star, but I play one in this book. Outside of this book I really am a doctor. My job is to help kids like you get better when they are feeling ill. Without a doubt, being sick can freak you out. But you don't need to be a doctor to calm yourself down. All you need is your own brain. The more you know about your illness, the less scary it will seem. That's why I always want my patients to understand how their bodies work. And that's why I'm here today.

Welcome to THE ADVENTURES OF MEDICAL MAN. Get your tickets ready, 'cause we're going to the movies. You see, I know that imagining what's going on inside your body can be difficult. It's much easier to enjoy a movie. So I've stepped up to star in five minor motion pictures—plus one comic book—that I hope will help you understand six common kid sicknesses. So make some popcorn, sit back, and enjoy our feature presentations. They're the feel-better movies of the year!

INSIDIOUS INVASION
NUT ALLERGY

At the dawn of the 21st century, who would have believed that life itself could be threatened by what seemed to be the most innocent of living things? And yet just such a threat occurred on the 30th day of last October. And, most shocking of all, it happened at a facility that prided itself on dealing with weird and unexpected dangers—the National Unusual Things Station.

Here at this secret outpost, the country's top military and scientific minds study the skies, ever watchful and ready for signs of trouble. This particular day started quietly, as so many days had before. The only odd thing prior to the fateful event was the presence of two children in the main observation hall. They were following lantern-jawed young doctor Mike Daring, the facility's chief medical expert, as they strolled past radar consoles and telescopes, toiling scientists and bustling soldiers.

"Gee, Dr. Daring, thanks for inviting us on a tour," said the boy. His eyes went wide at the sight of a towering telescope near the room's domed ceiling. The girl, meanwhile, squinted at the five-story screen overhead. It blinked with readouts and maps of the solar system.

"My pleasure, Billy," replied the doctor, patting him on the back. "As your and Sally's doctor, my job is to keep your bodies healthy. And one of the best ways to do that is to keep your minds healthy and inquisitive." The good doctor's

grin shrank when he spotted a straight-backed figure in uniform marching toward them. Dr. Daring leaned down to the children and whispered, "Don't let General Patent alarm you. His bark is worse than his bite."

The general came to a halt and puffed out his medal-laden chest. He glared at the trio. "I see you've once again brought children into my top-secret facility, Doctor."

"The only secret here is why we don't encourage more people to be curious about the world around them, General."

The general let out a sigh, his chest dropping with a jangle of his military awards. "You're right, of course. Anyway, nothing unusual ever happens here at the National Unusual Things Station. It's more science than soldiering, to be sure. Here, children, have a candy bar."

Unable to resist the lure of chocolate, Billy sprang forward with a grin. "Thanks!" In a flash he had torn open the wrapper and bitten into the sweet candy inside. Sally only frowned at the confection.

"Why, General," Dr. Daring said with a

wink, "I do believe that all these years of peace and quiet have finally convinced you there is nothing to fear. What could be safer than being in the National Unusual Things Station?"

It was at that moment that the fickle finger of fate chose to jab the station's calm. An ear-bursting emergency Klaxon pierced the air, and the bustling activity of hundreds of hands came to a halt. Heads turned and eyes stared up toward the young scientist at the eyepiece of the giant telescope. One of her fingers was still stabbing at the big red master alarm button on a nearby console. Sheet-white and trembling, she cried down to them, "I was looking at Mars. They—they came from Mars!"

"Put it on the main screen!" barked General Patent. The maps vanished and were replaced by an image of the red planet. Gasps and strangled screams escaped the lips of those around the room. On the screen an army of eight-legged, multi-eyed creatures writhed into view.

"Red alert!" barked the general.

"Oh dear," muttered Dr. Daring.

"Hmm." Sally frowned.

"I don't feel so good," moaned Billy.

Is Earth earmarked for annihilation by an alien army of oversized arachnids? Can our trio triumph over extraterrestrial tyranny? Does this story line have anything to do with a childhood illness? Find out by tuning in to the next episode of "They Came from Mars!"

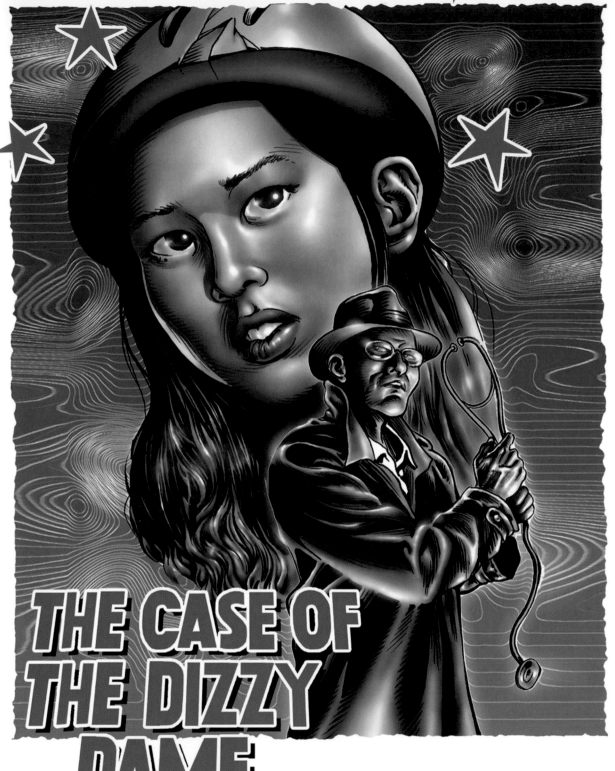

THE CASE OF THE DIZZY DAME

...A STORY AS BLUNT AS THE HEAD INJURY THAT INSPIRED IT!

FEATURING DR. MIKE EVANS AS MIKE DANGER, M.D., P.I.

The Case of the Dizzy Dame
CONCUSSION

It was a rainy Tuesday when she walked into my office. I could tell right away she was not your typical dizzy dame. Yeah, she was dizzy, but the scratches on her bicycle helmet told me it wasn't from being short on smarts. She told me she had a case. Nothing gets my wheels spinning like a mystery. I'm a gumshoe and I carry a bag—a doctor's bag. I'm Mike Danger, M.D., private investigator.

I sat her down and poured us two stiff ginger ales. I took mine neat. She took ice—for her head. She told me she'd lost her wheels: two of them, as in bicycle. She'd had a run-in with an oak tree. Next thing she knew, she was outside my office, but her bike was absent without leave. She thought it had been stolen. I thought she might be barking up the wrong tree.

I pulled out a folder and started a case file. "Where were you headed?" I asked with a click of my pen.

"Into the oak tree," she said. "Good thing I was wearing my helmet."

"I mean, what was your destination?" I pushed, but that one was a real head-scratcher. She couldn't recall.

I switched gears. "What day is today?" When she guessed Saturday, I knew this case had gone to her head. I told her that the news was both good and bad: her bike likely wasn't stolen, but she had been hurt in the crash.

"I do have a headache," she admitted. "But, Dr. Danger, if my bike hasn't been swiped, why do I feel so sick about it being missing?"

"Wanting to throw up can be a sign of wayward wheels," I conceded, "but matched with the other clues—memory loss and headache—a more likely suspect here is mild **concussion**."

"Miles who?" she asked, shifting her ice pack. I could see this would take some explaining.

"Not who, ma'am—what. Concussion can happen when your head takes a blow. Imagine this office is your skull and these filing cabinets are your brain." I tucked her folder into a filing drawer and stepped out into the hall.

"When you bump your head," I called to her, "it's like hitting the outer wall of the office." I get a kick out of demonstrating this concept,

The Unusual Suspects

When someone is not feeling well, it's a doctor's job to figure out what the problem might be. It's like a mystery with clues to be discovered. The most important clues are the sick person's history and **symptoms**: Where on the body is the problem? How does it feel—itchy, painful, swollen, achy? What have you been doing lately?

The doctor finds these clues by asking the patient (and sometimes the parents) questions: Have you felt this way before? Have you been around any sick people? What were you doing when you first felt sick? Does this hurt? Do you feel like throwing up? The doctor also finds clues by giving the patient a **physical examination**, a face-to-face meeting to look at and feel the area of sickness.

Like a detective, the doctor must put all these clues together. He or she knows about many illnesses and will find one that matches all the clues. The illness that fits the most clues becomes the prime suspect.

Once a prime suspect has been fingered, the doctor will run one or more tests on the patient. Each test is designed to look for proof of a specific illness. If the test doesn't produce proof, it's back to pounding the pavement: the doctor has to look at the clues again and find a new suspect—a different sickness that matches the clues.

When a test does prove that a specific illness is guilty, the doctor makes a **diagnosis**. Diagnosis comes from the Greek word for "recognize." The doctor has picked out the sickness present in the patient like a criminal in a police lineup. Once the doctor has the right diagnosis, he or she will know what treatments will most likely make the patient feel better and get healthy again.

and so does the wall. I gave it a mighty boot, and the two filing cabinets on the other side tumbled like the pizza boxes stacked on top of them. The lady winced.

"Your brain bounces off one side of your **skull** and then maybe the other," I said, stepping back into the room. File folders were all over the floor. "These folders are like your memories—the harder the hit, the more scrambled they can get."

I pulled her case file from the pile. "The memories surrounding the time when you got hurt are the first to get mixed up." I righted the first cabinet and began refiling the folders. "It takes the brain a while to get reorganized. It can take a few weeks. Some files can even be lost for good."

The other cabinet was pinned beneath some buckled plaster. "If the skull is cracked by the blow, it can cause bleeding that pushes on the brain. Which part of the brain

gets pressured will affect the way your body works." I picked up a pile of fallen photographs and a busted tape recorder. "If it's the part that operates your eyes, you may not able to see properly. The swelling could affect the part of your brain that operates hearing or talking."

Now I tried to lift the cabinet, but I could tell I'd need to fix that wall first, which could take some time. "Serious concussions can take longer to heal. However severe the concussion is, it's important for a doctor to keep an eye on you to make sure your symptoms are getting better, not worse. The doc may ask you questions, get you to exercise, have your head scanned to see if anything's broken, or even drain off any fluid, including blood, so it doesn't press on your brain."

"I was headed to the bike shop to get my brakes tuned up!" she suddenly remembered.

"Bad brakes … that's a bad break, but a good sign that you're already getting better," I said. "Even so, we'll have to make sure your parents check in on you every hour."

"Why's that?" she asked and gulped down her ginger ale.

"It's important to make sure your brain is reorganizing itself on its own. If things are getting more scrambled we need to know as soon as possible before your brain gets too scrambled for doctors to help. Come on, I'll drive you home."

"But what about my bike?" she asked.

I jerked open the blinds and nodded out the window. "We'll take it from that trunk and put it in mine." Right outside was a burly oak tree and beside it lay a mangled ten-speed. Case closed.

Double Fluidity

The skull is the perfect hideout for your brain. The bones of your skull are hard living tissue that protects your brain when your head gets a knock (when you wear a helmet, that hideout is even better protected). But did you know that your brain is also protected by liquid inside your skull?

Between your brain and your skull bones is a watery substance called **cerebrospinal fluid**, or CSF. This stuff keeps your brain from scraping against its walls as you move around in your daily life. At the same time, CSF pulls double duty as a courier, sending important messages in the form of **hormones** to your brain and **nervous system**. Not bad for a seemingly wishy-washy liquid.

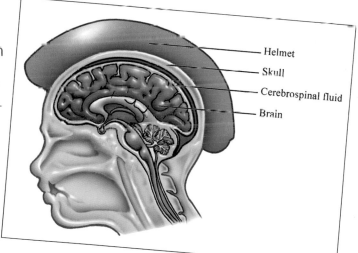

Helmet
Skull
Cerebrospinal fluid
Brain

NUT ALLERGY

When last we left Dr. Daring and his young friends, Earth seemed to be under imminent attack by giant spiders from Mars. Perhaps vexed by the vicious invasion, Billy had confessed to feeling ill. Now we rejoin our troubled trio at the National Unusual Things Station, where the panic is escalating …

*A*s the eight-legged antagonists loomed large on the overhead screen, soldiers and scientists ran in every direction. General Patent had found several phones and was hollering into all of them.

Dr. Daring was more concerned about Billy. "I can't do much about alien invaders, but a sick child is right up my alley. What ails you, my boy?"

Billy scratched at his cheeks, which were breaking out in an angry red **rash**. "I'm itchy and my stomach feels weird."

"We'd better get you to my lab upstairs." But even as he spoke, Dr. Daring spotted obstacles to his simple plan. Scientists were scurrying this way and that. An army of soldiers was charging into the room. Too many bustling bodies blocked the path to the medical stairwell. Billy was starting to sway slightly.

"What's wrong with him, Doctor?" cried Sally as she dodged a squealing scramble of scientists.

As Dr. Daring ducked the bulky backpack of a passing trooper, he spotted the crumpled candy wrapper on the floor. He snatched it up and showed it to Sally. "I fear the lad is having an allergic reaction to something he ate."

"Nuts!" cried Sally.

"No need to curse—we'll get through this," Dr. Daring assured her.

"No, Doctor, I think Billy is allergic to nuts!" shouted Sally, taking shelter behind an office chair from the onrushing troops.

"Almonds … " Billy wheezed. "Medicine … in my bag."

"We had to leave our bags at the security desk!" gasped Sally.

"My lab is closer," announced Dr. Daring. "But we'll need to get him there quickly."

Sally leapt to her feet and pulled the rolling chair over to Billy. "Get on!" she ordered, and he stumbled into the seat. She looked despairingly at the panicked mob and then at the screen, where the monstrous forms continued to wriggle.

"Is Billy going to be okay?" Sally yelled to Dr. Daring as she pursued him along a corridor beside some cubicles.

"Nut allergies are like an alien invasion," Dr. Daring called back, glancing at the screen above. "Your body labels the nut as a UFO—an unidentified foreign object. In other words, it's an **allergen**. Your body mistakes the allergen for something harmful and reacts to defend itself. If you're a kid with allergies, you have an extra-powerful immune system. An allergic attack is when your body's immune system overreacts. Some overreactions show up as mild symptoms, such as a rash or a cough, while other over-reactions are more serious—even life-threatening."

The trio skidded to a stop at a cubicle crossroads. A skinny, sweating scientist blocked their path. "You're not authorized to be in this area," he screeched, waving his walkie-talkie. "I'll have to report you!"

"One type of reaction is a rash, also known as **hives**," Dr. Daring explained, looking around him. "This can happen, as it has with Billy, when you eat the allergen. It can even happen on skin that has simply touched the allergen. A rash can be irritating, even painful, but it will go away on its own." His eyes fell upon a fire extinguisher hanging on the wall.

"Your doctor can recommend creams, lotions, ointments, or even pills that will make your skin feel better until the rash disappears," Dr. Daring assured them as he pulled the extinguisher free. With a wink and a *whoosh*, he unleashed a spray of foam at the gangly guard, sending him scurrying away with a shriek. Dr. Daring blew the excess foam from the nozzle and hooked the extinguisher on his belt. "Come on!"

On they ran as the station's public address system crackled to life and General Patent's voice filled the hall. "Intruder alert reported! All nonmilitary personnel are to be removed from the observation hall—now!"

Just ahead of the trio, two burly troopers pointed in their direction.

"I don't like the look of this," Sally gulped.

Are our agile action stars on the outs with the officials? Might lifesaving medication for Billy be delayed by the mayhem? Stay tuned for the next episode of "They Came from Mars!"

Chemical Warfare

The human body is designed to protect itself from invasion by infectious **germs** or **viruses**. When your body detects the presence of something that might harm it, it alerts the **immune system**, which responds by releasing **infection**-fighting chemicals into your blood. These chemicals are called **antibodies**.

One type of antibody is called immunoglobulin E, or IgE. IgE antibodies find the invaders and latch on to them. Once the invader is in its grip, IgE releases chemicals called **histamines**. Histamines do two things:

1. They prepare the way for the big guns of body defense—the **white blood cells**.
2. They can mess with the normal operations of your skin, stomach, lungs, and even blood flow.

In other words, while histamines help fight infection, they can also give you symptoms like itchy skin, upset stomach, runny nose, and light-headedness. Sound familiar? That's because this chemical warfare is going on when you have a cold or an **allergy** attack.

You might hear cold and allergy medications referred to as **antihistamines**. These are medicines designed to reduce the histamines in your body.

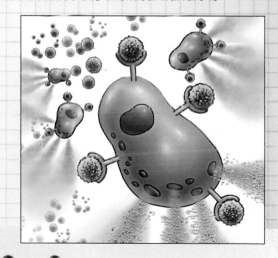

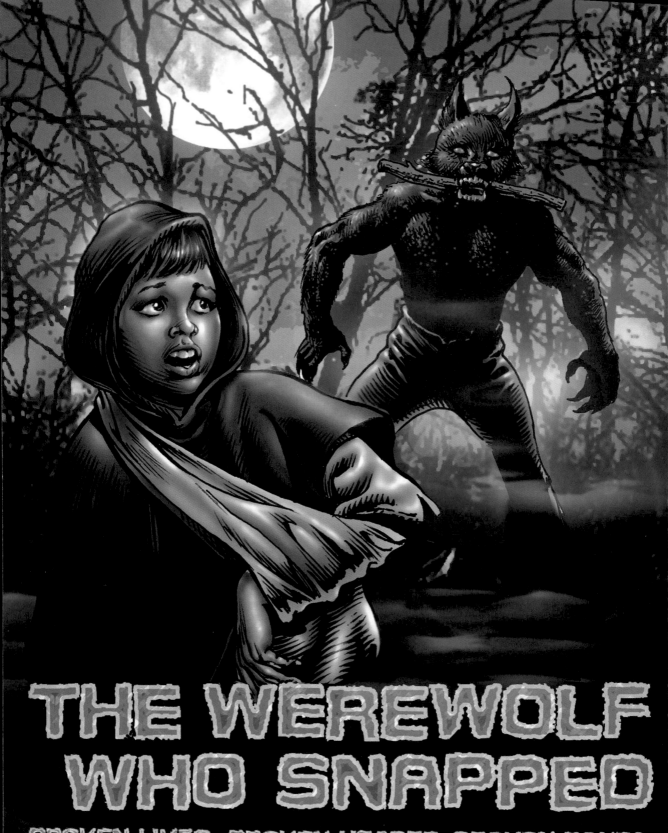

THE WEREWOLF WHO SNAPPED

BROKEN LIVES. BROKEN HEARTS. BROKEN BONES.

STARRING DR. MIKE EVANS AS DR. MICHAEL VAN LYSANDER

The Werewolf Who Snapped

BROKEN BONES

Believe me when I tell you that werewolves are real. For generations my family has committed themselves to the hunting of these nocturnal creatures. Although most times these beasts walk the earth as men, it takes only the caress of a silvery moon at its peak to turn them into snarling, savage monsters. Such were the conditions one chilly night when I and a village companion tracked a former patient of mine into the woods. A doctor by day, I, too, have a second identity that reveals itself at the full moon: I am Dr. Michael van Lysander, hunter of werewolves.

My companion this night was a maiden named Lucy. Though her looks were fair, her demeanor was as hard and sharp as the bitter wind. And little wonder, for the beast we tracked was, in times less harried, her older brother. I had vowed to take him without injury and keep him thus unharmed until the moon had passed its phase. Alas, Lucy's fate was not to escape equally unscathed.

We had just forded an icy stream and were clambering up the far bank. Anxious that the water might have left the trail cold, I raised my torch high and spotted telltale scratches on the trunk of young sapling ahead. With a bellow, I hastened the girl to follow me thither. But in her excitement she slipped on a rock slick with frost and took a tumble down the bank. In a heartbeat I was by her side. As I took her arm to help her to her feet, she cried out. The limb was damaged, and we could go no farther until it was tended.

The sapling I had seen revealed itself to be one of a family that framed a clearing at the top of the bank. There I built a fire to keep young Lucy warm and to give me better light by which to work. Carefully I pulled back the sleeve of her tunic and examined the offended limb. By the light of the fire I could see that the arm was swollen near the elbow. Fortunately there was no blood, the scent of which I feared would draw the beast. Upon my inquiring as to her sensations, she admitted to considerable discomfort and a feeling of pins and needles pricking her fingers. And indeed, those **phalanges** responded with little movement when she tried to move them.

I had hoped it was just a **sprain**, the solution for which would have been a simple **sling** that would allow us to continue on our adventure. But Lucy's difficulty moving her fingers indicated the possibility of a broken bone, which could not risk being jostled. Only lashing the limb to two solid sticks—an application called a **splint**—would do. Once that was done, we would have to make haste back to my laboratory and its **X-ray** machine to confirm a break. I told her this news.

"Can you be certain it is not just a sprain?" Lucy pleaded. She was eager, I knew, to continue the hunt for her brother.

"You are young, Lucy," I began. "Among the fully grown, bones tend to be harder, stronger." I picked up my sturdy torch (now extinguished), its wood hardened by the heat, and demonstrated its inflexible constitution. "Such bones better withstand a fall, but the **ligaments**, **tendons**, and muscles are more likely to strain or tear."

Now I picked up the branch of a sapling, still green with youth. "Your young bones are more flexible, and more apt to break." I held the branch at each end and bent it. In moments it was splintered in the middle, revealing threadlike strands of green wood inside, but not fully breaking apart.

I held the splintered stick aloft for her to see. "This type of fracture is a very classic of its kind. In fact, it bears the name **greenstick fracture**. Do you see how one side is splintered but the other has stayed intact?"

Lucy nodded, her jaw set and her brow furrowed in the firelight. "Is that what has happened to the bone in my arm?"

"That is impossible to say without my X-ray apparatus." I frowned. Tossing the splintered stick deep into the woods, I picked up another. "It could be a **simple fracture**: a single break in the bone with little damage to the surrounding tissue or skin." I produced my handkerchief and wrapped it around the new stick as though it were skin. Then I broke the branch in twain, ensuring that the cloth stayed intact. "See? Not a tear." I tossed the two halves into the forest.

I picked up another branch and broke it into three pieces. "More than two breaks to the bone is a **comminuted fracture**." Lucy's eyes grew wide and her mouth fell agape. "Yes, it can be quite shocking to think about," I admitted. "But that's not the least of it."

Strangely, I found that one of my earlier demonstration branches had found its way back to my feet. I brought it down hard, point first, onto a rock, and the stick buckled near the middle. "A **compression fracture** comes from an impact such as jumping from too great a height. No need to look so startled, my dear. That is a more likely fate for the legs or the spine. You also needn't fear this next, most chilling of fractures."

The original sapling branch had somehow come to be once more by my side. I seized it now and snapped it completely apart. Lucy's lips spread into a slow smile. Given the graphic nature of my explanations, I feared the poor thing was going into shock, but I pressed on.

"An **open**, or **compound**, **fracture** causes the bone to actually protrude through the skin!" With that, I stabbed half the stick through my handkerchief until it tore through to the other side. Lucy began to giggle. "It's no laughing matter, my dear! It is, in fact, a nasty business and prone to infection. But as we can see, your arm shows no signs of such damage."

Despite my attempts to convey the gravity of the situation, the poor girl seemed positively delighted. With growing impatience I tossed the sticks aside once more. Drawing a deep breath, I prepared to lecture Lucy sternly on the importance of knowing the facts in medical matters.

Before I could begin, however, a low whine from behind me caught my attention. I froze as the sound was followed by heavy panting. Despite the roaring flames, my skin turned to ice. Slowly I turned. There by the firelight stood the werewolf. In its fierce and dripping jaws was clutched a collection of broken sticks. The beast spat the branches upon the ground and let out a barking roar that chilled me to my own solid bones. Whether it then cast a blow at me or its powers extended to the psychic, I cannot say, but whatever the cause, I lost my conscious awareness and all turned to black.

When I awoke, I was on the cot in my laboratory and the morning sun was shining through the window. At my

side was Lucy, her arm neatly encased in a bright pink cast. Behind her stood her now-hairless brother in hospital scrubs. By day, it transpired, Lucy's brother is a fully trained X-ray technician. Using my equipment, he had been able to confirm that her injury was indeed a greenstick fracture.

As for Lucy's cast, it had been prepared by my laboratory colleague, who had diagnosed my own condition as a simple fainting spell. I'm not so sure about that, but the cast was indeed fine work. The next time I see my fellow medical practioner, I must be sure to thank the good Dr. Jekyll.

NIGHT OF THE LIVING TISSUE

Skeletons may be a symbol of scary dead people, but don't be fooled—your bones are as alive as the rest of you. They are made up of living **tissue** that continues to grow your whole life. When you were born, you had almost 270 different bones in your body. By the time you're an adult that number will be down to 206. Where do the extra bones go? They don't go—they grow. As you get older, some of those bones grow into one another until they fuse into a single bone.

All that growing is good news if you break a bone. A cracked bone can mend itself, but it does need help. First, the bone must be **set**. With the help of an X-ray image, a doctor will carefully arrange the broken ends into the best position to heal properly. It's important to hold the bone in that position while the tissue slowly grows back together. Holding it still is easier when you use a **cast**—a large, stiff bandage that covers the area where the bone is broken. The inside of the cast is a soft material that will be comfortable against your skin. The outside is a hard material such as fiberglass or plaster, which keeps the bone from shifting and helps the healing. Right after a fracture, your body usually swells up. This swelling is your body making its own cast. Until this swelling goes down, your doctor may give you a temporary cast.

GASTROINTESTINAL GRIEF

NUT ALLERGY

It was a dangerous day for Dr. Daring and his young mates. The threat of alien invasion had caused chaos in the National Unusual Things Station. Mistaken for intruders, our heroes were set upon by single-minded soldiers, even as the clock ticked down on Billy's deteriorating health …

7he two burly soldiers lumbered their way over to our troubled trio. "You heard the general's orders," the bigger soldier growled. "It's time for you three to leave."

Dr. Daring waved his medical badge. "Stand down, trooper! I have a sick patient who needs immediate medical attention."

"Nope," grunted the other grunt. "Orders are orders."

A smirk appeared on the good doctor's face. Faster than a reflex hammer can bop your knee and make it kick, Dr. Daring had drawn his trusty extinguisher and squeezed the trigger. But nothing emerged except a disappointing *squish* of air.

Dr. Daring frowned and whispered to Billy, "A more serious allergic reaction can happen when an allergenic food reaches your stomach. Like these guards, your stomach will do everything it can to get rid of what's bothering it. You might throw up the food, or you might get **diarrhea** as your body tries to flush the allergen out the other end. Or you might experience both."

By _____   Date _____

Gross Encounters
of the Food Kind

Gastro means stomach and *intestinal* means guts. Put them together and you've got the **gastrointestinal** (or **digestive**) **system**. Food takes a journey through that system when you eat, and it's quite a trip. From your mouth your meal goes down your **esophagus**, the tube that leads to the stomach. In your stomach that chewed-up food and drink mix with your **gastric juices**—the liquids your stomach uses to further mush up food until it is ready to drain into your guts, where the real action happens.

The chief gut in the digestive system is your **large intestine**—"large" because if you stretched it out it would measure about 1.5 meters (5 feet). It's here that your body sucks the **nutrients** out of that mushed-up food, and those nutrients are the fuel that keeps your body running. (Foods that your parents say are good for you contain super-charged body fuel. Junk food can taste good, but is lousy fuel.) Once the digested food has reached the end of the large intestine, all the nutrients have been removed. At this point it's no longer food—now it's poop. Your body has no more use for it, so it's ready to be dumped in the nearest convenient toilet.

That's how the system is supposed to work. But sometimes something can get into your stomach that your body doesn't like. It could be **bacteria**, a virus, or it could be food you are allergic to. When this happens, the intestine tries to push the eject button. The muscles in your stomach that normally pull food down push it back up instead—that's what happens when you throw up. If the invading bacteria or allergen makes it into your large intestine, it's too late to eject. Instead, your guts go into fast-forward. Your stomach and other organs pump liquids into your intestine to flush out your system, and for you that means diarrhea: a lot of wet poop, flowing fast and furious.

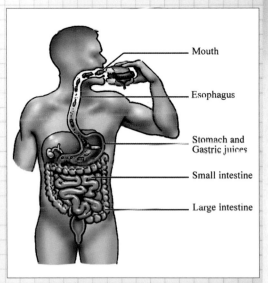

— Mouth

— Esophagus

— Stomach and Gastric juices

— Small intestine

— Large intestine

"That's enough out of you," sneered one of the soldiers as they advanced on the threatened three. Powerful hands grabbed the group and shoved them into a nearby escape tube.

Moments later, the tube spat the trio out an emergency exit and scattered them on the lawn of the National Unusual Things Station. A hatch behind them sealed with a hiss, cutting off the chaos inside. But the commotion outside was even louder. The nearby streets were packed with panicked people perturbed by the news of arachnid invaders. Lines of soldiers were vainly trying to restore order.

"We're locked out!" cried Sally, tugging at the hatch door. "Will Billy be all right if he just throws up, like you said?" she asked hopefully. "No medicine required?"

Dr. Daring scowled and crawled over to Billy, who was looking as green as the grass on which he now lay.

"Afraid not, Sally. Billy's body is responding seriously to the allergen. We have to respond just as seriously to that reaction before it can cause even worse problems," he cautioned.

"T-tear …" stammered Billy.

"That's right, Billy," Dr. Daring. "Watery eyes can be another reaction."

"… tear gas!" Billy finished. Sally and Dr. Daring followed his gaze toward the street, where, sure enough, the soldiers had released a cloud of tear gas to keep the marauding mob away from the National Unusual Things Station. Tendrils of gas snaked a smoky trail toward our trio.

"The wind is blowing the gas right at us!" Sally warned, already coughing. "We're doomed!"

Will the calamitous cloud cause our crew to be conquered by coughing? Can our friends break away from the tear gas and break in to the station before Billy has a breakdown? Find out on the next exciting episode of "They Came from Mars!"

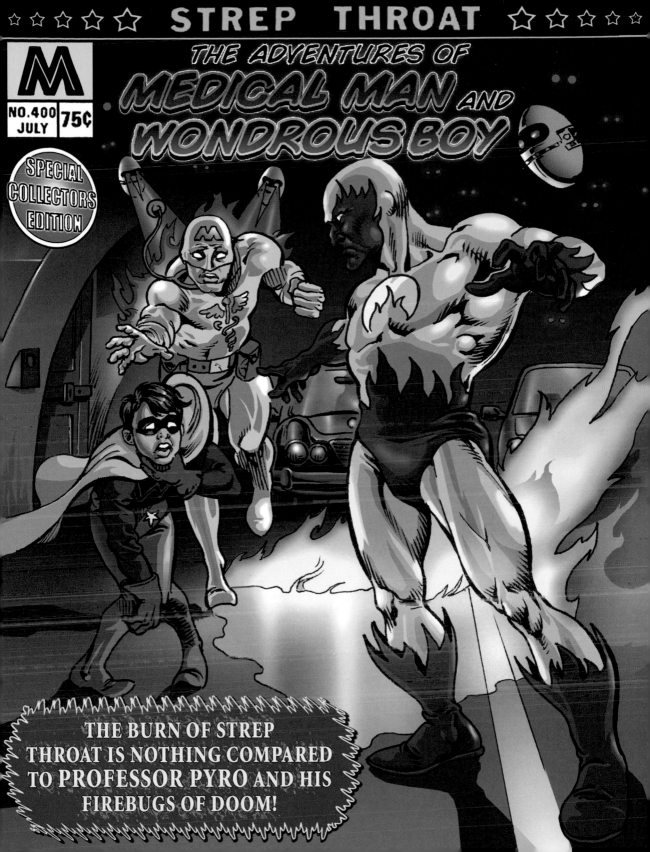

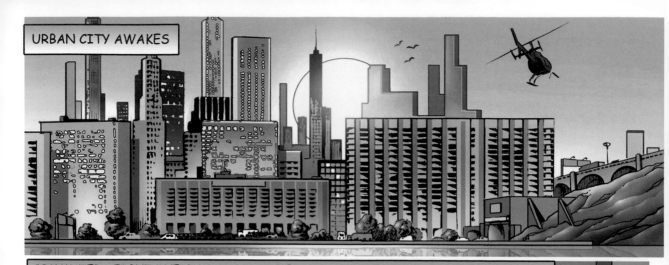

URBAN CITY AWAKES

COMMUTERS FIGHT THEIR WAY INTO THE CITY VIA THE RIVER STREET TUNNEL. LITTLE DO THEY KNOW THAT SOON THEY WILL BE FIGHTING MORE THAN TRAFFIC.

SOON THEY WILL BE FIGHTING FOR THEIR VERY LIVES.

SOON THEY WILL BE FIGHTING PROFESSOR PYRO AND HIS FIREBUGS OF DOOM!

ATTACK, MY PETS. GO FOR THEIR THROATS!

MEANWHILE, ACROSS TOWN DR. MIKE MICHAELS IS BATTLING BUGS OF A DIFFERENT KIND.

THIS SPIDER BITE IS NOTHING TO WORRY ABOUT, PETER.

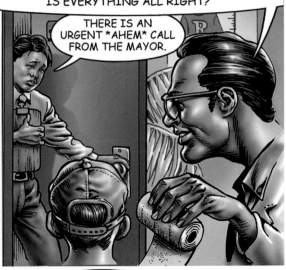

GRAY DIXON, MY RECEPTIONIST EXTRAORDINAIRE. IS EVERYTHING ALL RIGHT?

THERE IS AN URGENT *AHEM* CALL FROM THE MAYOR.

BY THE ROD OF ASCLEPIUS! I MUST GO!

PSST. DO WATCH THAT BITE FOR UNUSUAL SYMPTOMS.

VILLAINY NEVER SEEMS TO MAKE AN APPOINTMENT, GRAY.

CLICK WHIRR

FORTUNATELY FOR URBAN CITY, THERE IS ONE TEAM THAT IS ALWAYS ON CALL...

AHEM

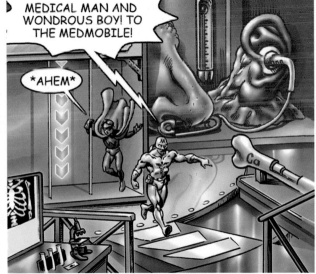

MEDICAL MAN AND WONDROUS BOY! TO THE MEDMOBILE!

AHEM

LOOKS LIKE TROUBLE AT THE *AHEM* RIVER STREET TUNNEL.

THE TUNNEL IS OFTEN CONGESTED AT THIS HOUR.

SPEAKING OF CONGESTION, ARE YOU HAVING TROUBLE WITH YOUR THROAT?

GREAT ACHING GLOTTIS, MEDICAL MAN! IT FEELS LIKE MY THROAT IS ON FIRE! I'M ALSO HOT AND ACHY.

HMM, MOST LIKELY A COMMON **VIRUS**. BUT IT ALSO COULD BE A MORE SERIOUS **STREPTOCOCCUS** INFECTION. I'D BETTER TAKE A LOOK.

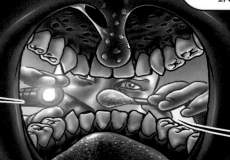

YOUR **TONSILS** ARE ENLARGED AND RED AND PRODUCING **PUS**. * THERE ARE ALSO SPOTS IN YOUR MOUTH.

IT LOOKS LIKE IT MAY BE **STREP THROAT**, ALL RIGHT. I'LL TAKE A **SWAB** TO BE SURE.

* FOR MORE ON PUS, SEE THE AD ON PAGE 35- ED.

85% OF SORE THROATS ARE CAUSED BY VIRUSES, **NOT** STREP BACTERIA. DOCTORS PREDICT IF IT'S STREP WITH A SCORING SYSTEM: YOU GET ONE POINT EACH FOR HAVING A FEVER, SWOLLEN NODES ON THE FRONT OF YOUR NECK, PUS ON YOUR TONSILS, **NOT** HAVING A COUGH, AND BEING UNDER AGE 15. A SCORE OF ZERO OR ONE MEANS YOU DON'T HAVE STREP. A SCORE OF FIVE STILL MEANS ONLY A 51% CHANCE YOU HAVE IT. ONLY A LAB TEST CAN SHOW FOR SURE.

YES, STREPTOCOCCUS BACTERIA ARE CLEARLY GROWING HERE. YOU DO HAVE STREP THROAT.

IT'S *AHEM* BACTERIA FIGHTING TIME!

DING!

FOOLS! ONLY I CAN STOP MY FIRE-BUGS FROM CHOKING TRAFFIC.

ALL YOU'LL GET IS A BLAST FROM MY COUGH OF COMBUSTION!

HOW DID I GET THIS STREP THROAT, ANYWAY?

STREPTOCOCCI ARE BACTERIA. IF SOMEONE WITH THOSE BACTERIA COUGHS OR SNEEZES NEAR YOU, THE GERMS CAN TRAVEL INTO YOUR BODY.

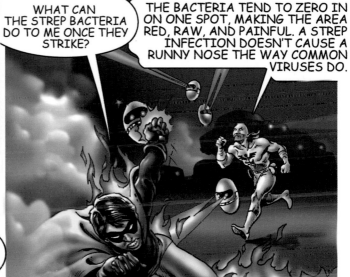

WHAT CAN THE STREP BACTERIA DO TO ME ONCE THEY STRIKE?

THE BACTERIA TEND TO ZERO IN ON ONE SPOT, MAKING THE AREA RED, RAW, AND PAINFUL. A STREP INFECTION DOESN'T CAUSE A RUNNY NOSE THE WAY COMMON VIRUSES DO.

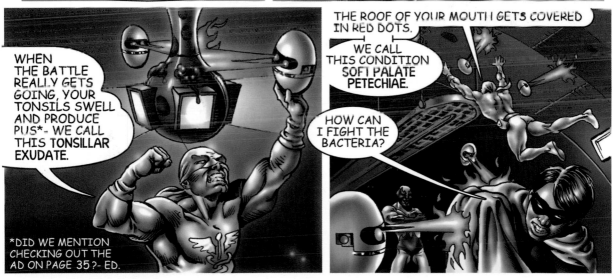

WHEN THE BATTLE REALLY GETS GOING, YOUR TONSILS SWELL AND PRODUCE PUS*- WE CALL THIS TONSILLAR EXUDATE.

THE ROOF OF YOUR MOUTH GETS COVERED IN RED DOTS.

WE CALL THIS CONDITION SOFT PALATE PETECHIAE.

HOW CAN I FIGHT THE BACTERIA?

*DID WE MENTION CHECKING OUT THE AD ON PAGE 35 ?- ED.

OUR BODY'S IMMUNE SYSTEM TRIES TO FIGHT THE INFECTION. THE BATTLE BEGINS IN OUR **LYMPH NODES**, CAUSING THEM TO SWELL. YOU ALSO GET A FEVER.

WHAT HAPPENS IF MY IMMUNE SYSTEM CAN'T FIGHT OFF THE INFECTION?

DOCTORS CAN EFFECTIVELY USE **ANTIBIOTICS*** TO HELP YOUR BODY WIN THE FIGHT AGAINST BACTERIA.

*WHAT ARE ANTIBIOTICS? SEE PAGE 37- ED.

ANTIBIOTICS CAN BE TAKEN AS A SINGLE SHOT THAT BEGINS WORKING RIGHT AWAY.....

CLANG

...OR AS PILLS THAT ARE TAKEN DAILY FOR A WHILE.

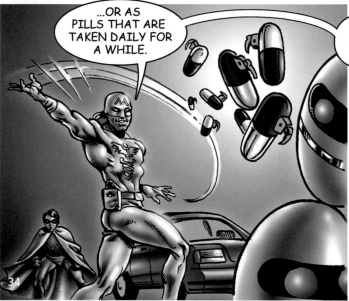

IT IS VERY IMPORTANT THAT YOU TAKE YOUR ANTIBIOTICS AS DIRECTED SO THE INFECTION DOESN'T COME BACK OR BECOME MORE RESISTANT.

ENTER THE WONDERFUL WORLD OF AMAZING PUS

Do you have a bacterial infection AND a strong stomach? If so, now you can grow your very own pus in the comfort of your own body.

It can be yellow!
It can be green!
It can be brown!
It can be white!
Whatever the color, pus is a thick liquid that appears wherever living tissue battles invading bacteria.

Inside that liquid you'll find

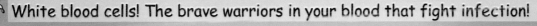

White blood cells! The brave warriors in your blood that fight infection!

Dead bacteria! The fallen enemy agents that made you sick in the first place!

Dead tissue! Bits of once-living cells that didn't survive the bacterial onslaught!

This is a limited-time offer! If you see pus and redness forming around a cut, you may have an infection that needs medical attention!

Charles Abscess, M.D.

Hey, SICKY! Bullied by bacteria? Your doctor can help YOU fight off infection with ANTIBIOTICS.

Are you sick of being pushed around by bacterial infections like strep throat? Don't you wish there was a medicine you could take to get rid of those single-celled tyrants? There is!

Antibiotics are a special kind of medicine that targets the bacteria that are making you sick. Like many medicines, antibiotics can come in different forms: pills, liquid drops, creams, ointments, or even a needle from your doctor.

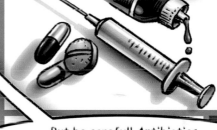

But be careful! Antibiotics won't help you with a sickness that is NOT caused by bacteria. If you use them when they're not needed, your body will build up an immunity to them, making them less effective. That's why only a health care professional can prescribe antibiotics. Not available off the shelf in stores.

AISLE 7
ANTIBIOTICS

Episode 4
They Came From Mars!

NUT ALLERGY

Danger was all around! Our troubled trio had been ejected from the National Unusual Things Station only to face an approaching cloud of noxious tear gas. Worse still, the medicine Billy needed was back in the building. Could our heroes find a way back in and away from the gas?

"Up there!" shouted Dr. Daring, pointing at the building. Sally and Billy looked up and saw a series of people-sized clear tubes leading down from the roof. "That fire escape should take us to the second-floor hallway. My lab is at the far end."

Sally was already reloading Billy onto the office chair. Dr. Daring helped her push it across the grass as they fled the tear gas wafting their way. As they reached the base of the fire escape, Sally spotted a box containing a fire hose. In moments she had its door open, the hose unreeled, and a spray of water dousing the corrosive cloud.

"Good thinking, Sally!" Dr. Daring whooped. "That reminds me of how your body's **respiratory system** can react to allergens. *Respiration* is a fancy word for breathing, and your respiratory system includes all the parts of your body that help you breathe: the airways that lead from your nose and mouth to your lungs, as well as the muscles that help move oxygen around. When your body senses something in an airway that it doesn't like—such as tear gas or an allergen—it will try to keep it out. Your nose might run and your eyes might water. That's your body trying to drain out the invader."

Sally let out a cheer as the cloud shrank from the force of the fire hose. She dropped the nozzle and joined Dr. Daring, who was struggling to haul Billy and his chair up into the fire-escape tube. Together they managed to lug the bulky bundle of Billy toward the second-story landing.

All at once, a new siren sounded. At the top of the tube appeared a robot eye on a metallic stalk.

"I don't like the sound of that," muttered Sally.

A tinny voice announced, "INTRUDER ALERT, WEST FIRE ESCAPE. ACTIVATING SECURITY RESTRICTIONS." With a whir, the fire-escape tube began to narrow.

"Tight squeeze," gasped Dr. Daring. "Which is what can happen when your body's airways react to an allergen. The muscles swell, narrowing the passages."

A loud *clunk* was heard as nozzles appeared at the top of the tube and began to rain down a sticky liquid.

Dr. Daring continued: "When the body's intruder repulsion system goes overboard, it also produces **mucus** to block the invader. When these defenses also block oxygen from getting through, it's an **asthma** attack. Such attacks can be mild but they can also be the most dangerous kind of reaction."

"No kidding," spat Sally as goop oozed and the walls constricted.

"This reminds me of that movie *Asthmatic Mike and the Temple of Wheeze*," gasped Billy.

"It reminds me of whistling,"

Dr. Daring replied. He pursed his lips together and sounded a few notes. "When we whistle, we constrict our lips to make a smaller opening for the air to pass through. When we wheeze, it's because the airways in our lungs are getting smaller."

Thinking quickly, Dr. Daring wiggled the fire extinguisher free from his belt and jammed it across the tube, stopping the walls from narrowing any further. Then he aimed its hose at the sticky-liquid nozzles overhead and squeezed the trigger. The empty extinguisher emitted a stream of air right into the electronic eye, and it let out a robotic shriek and disappeared. As the extinguisher continued to emit air, the ooze began to evaporate.

"This extinguisher is acting like an **inhaler**, a device that administers medication directly into your airways," Dr. Daring explained as the goop dried up. "The medicine encourages your body to relax the constricting muscles so air can get through again." And with that the good doctor was able to wiggle forward and pop out onto the second-story landing. Quickly he helped pull Billy and Sally free after him.

"Are we there yet?" Billy groaned.

A fair question, Billy. Have our heroes fared well and finally reached a place to rest? Or is their welfare at an end as they face their final resting place? Stay tuned for the next episode of "They Came from Mars!"

THE HURT IS ON

THE HURT FROM RED EARDRUM

With Dr. Mike Evans as Captain Mike deBoot

EAR INFECTION

Ocean, ocean, and more ocean. All is quiet even after 60 days at sea—under it, actually—and my crew grows restless. This boredom, plus the tight confines of our submarine, has temperatures rising, and I don't mean tempers. This is Captain Mike deBoot reporting, and I fear that infection has stowed away aboard the *U-Station*.

My first officer, young Otis, came to me this morning complaining of pain in his ear. I asked him what the crew was giving him an earful about now, but he insisted that this ear discomfort was coming from the inside and not from his comrades.

"Up **otoscope**!" I ordered, and from my medical bag I produced the special instrument for looking into the ear. Gently I inserted the small end of its cone into Otis's ear, activated the light, and peered into the lens at the wide end.

Straight ahead I could see that Otis's **eardrum** was an angry red. With the otoscope I released a puff of air against the eardrum. It didn't wiggle as a healthy eardrum should. I put the instrument away and told Otis that I suspected an infection.

Otis swallowed hard, then winced. "How do you know it's an infection, sir?"

"Bring the sub to the surface," I ordered, "and I'll explain."

Minutes later, Otis and I stood on the *U-Station*'s conning tower, looking out over the calm sea. "Imagine the entire submarine is your head lying on its side," I said, "and this tower is your ear. Three compartments connect your ear to your brain: the **outer ear**, the **middle ear**, and the **inner ear**. Follow me."

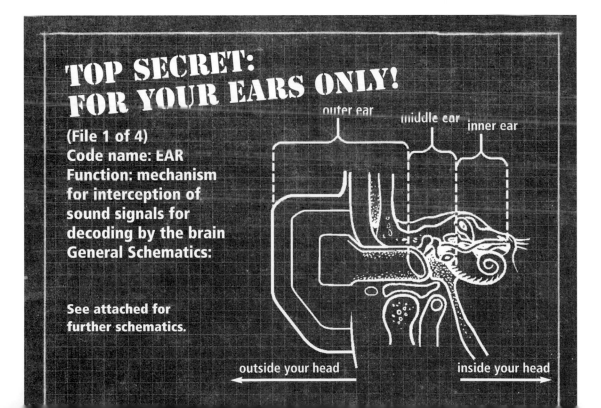

TOP SECRET: FOR YOUR EARS ONLY!

(File 1 of 4)
Code name: EAR
Function: mechanism for interception of sound signals for decoding by the brain
General Schematics:

See attached for further schematics.

outer ear   middle ear   inner ear

outside your head   inside your head

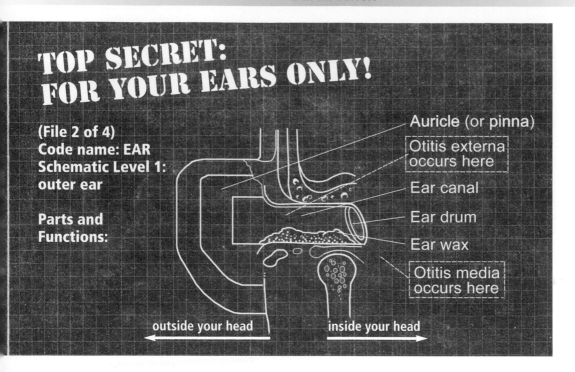

TOP SECRET: FOR YOUR EARS ONLY!

(File 2 of 4)
Code name: EAR
Schematic Level 1:
outer ear

Parts and
Functions:

Auricle (or pinna)

Otitis externa occurs here

Ear canal

Ear drum

Ear wax

Otitis media occurs here

outside your head ← → inside your head

We climbed back down the tower and began moving aft through the sub's tight central corridor.

"This hallway is the part of your outer ear called the **ear canal**." I grabbed a nearby bucket of grease and splashed it against the wall. Otis gaped. "Your ear canal is protected by a coating of **ear wax**, which keeps germs from sticking inside your ear." I tossed my chewing gum against the wall—it slid right off the grease. Otis nodded in understanding as I popped a fresh piece into my mouth.

"One type of infection is called **swimmer's ear**. Let me show you. Dive!" I ordered.

"But the top hatch is still open," Otis sputtered.

"Dive!" I ordered again, and as the *U-Station* dipped beneath the waves, water came pouring in from above. "Surface!" I soon gurgled, and the crew gratefully complied.

Soon the last of the water was trickling down the walls, washing the grease away. "Swimmer's ear is caused when water introduces things that like to grow, such as bacteria or fungus, into the ear canal, and washes away the ear wax." I spat out my gum and chucked it at the wall. This time it stuck.

"Ear wax is slightly acidic and moves any intruders out. Without it, intruders can stick and grow. As your body tries to fight off those germs, your ear canal swells up and becomes painful, and you may get a fever. Your body can usually fight off the bacteria on its own, though a doctor may give you ear drops and sometimes pills to help." With my pen I pried the gum off the wall and flicked it to the floor. "You should stay out of water until all the swelling and

pain are gone, to keep the new ear wax that your body makes from washing away again."

Otis tried to poke a finger in his ear, but I pulled his arm down. "And you should keep your fingers out of there! Fingers can add reinforcements to the bacteria. This kind of infection is officially called **otitis externa**, Otis. A doctor can see that you have it by looking for redness and swelling in the ear canal." I peeked again with my otoscope. "I don't see that in your ear."

Otis looked dejected. "So what do I have then?"

"I suspect a more common type of ear infection," I replied. "**Otitis media**—an infection of the middle ear. Follow me."

We stepped through the hatch into the crew quarters and stopped. I pulled the

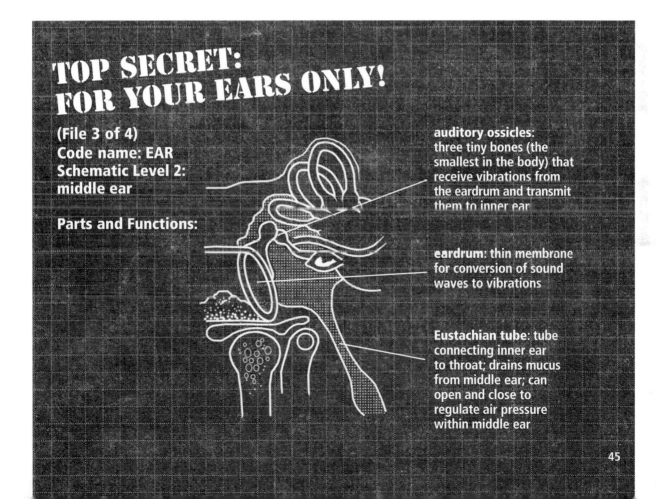

TOP SECRET: FOR YOUR EARS ONLY!

(File 3 of 4)
Code name: EAR
Schematic Level 2: middle ear

Parts and Functions:

auditory ossicles: three tiny bones (the smallest in the body) that receive vibrations from the eardrum and transmit them to inner ear

eardrum: thin membrane for conversion of sound waves to vibrations

Eustachian tube: tube connecting inner ear to throat; drains mucus from middle ear; can open and close to regulate air pressure within middle ear

privacy curtain into place. "The ear canal ends here, at the eardrum. It's a thin membrane of tissue that separates your outer ear from your middle ear. When it's healthy, it moves easily when you blow on it, as I did with the otoscope." I inhaled mightily and blew as hard as I could—the curtain rustled freely.

"But when your middle ear gets infected, it fills up with **pus**." I reached over and opened a valve on the wall. Otis's eyes went wide as water flooded into the compartment and quickly began to rise. Alarms rang out. I held the curtain shut as the water rose past our knees. When the curtain began to bulge outward, I turned the valve again and the water stopped. Otis looked relieved.

"The pus puts pressure on the eardrum and can clog up the **Eustachian tube** so the eardrum doesn't move as easily." I blew again, but this time the curtain remained taut as the waist-level water pushed against it. "This can be painful and can cause a fever. When your eardrum stops moving, it's not as good at hearing. Sometimes the pressure gets so great it can cause the eardrum to burst." I stabbed at the curtain with my pen. It tore easily and water poured out into the corridor. "When that happens, you may wake up to find **discharge** on your pillow. The good news is that because the pain is mostly due to pressure on the eardrum, the pain goes away when the pressure is relieved."

Otis clutched his ear and gaped at the ripped curtain. I pulled the torn edges back together. "Don't worry about a burst eardrum," I assured him. "It heals by itself."

I sloshed farther back into the compartment, where the water was draining more slowly. "See these drain pipes over here? These are like a tube in your middle ear called the Eustachian tube. It drains fluid such as mucus away from your ear and down into your throat."

I pointed to a wider pipe. "As we get older, our heads get bigger and our Eustachian tubes grow wider and more angled, allowing them to drain more easily." Turning yet another valve, I closed the wide drain pipe, leaving only a smaller pipe open. The draining water slowed almost to a stop—my partially chewed gum was clearly gumming up the tube. "But in kids younger than three, the tubes are still very small, and flat. They easily get clogged. If a young child gets a lot of infections because of those too-small tubes, a doctor may insert an artificial tube in the eardrum to drain the fluid and reduce the pressure in the middle ear." I inserted a wider section of pipe into the drain, removing the gummed-up bit. "Eventually those tubes fall out on their own as the child grows."

Otis gently touched his ear and looked worried. "So how do you treat it, sir?"

"Most ear infections are from viruses, not bacteria, so antibiotics won't help. The body is able to fight off the infection on its own approximately 85% of the time. If the body needs help because the infection is bacterial and not viral, a health care professional will prescribe antibiotics." I reopened the main drain and the water flowed away.

From the crew quarters we continued down the corridor, stopping finally at the communications room. "The final compartment is the inner ear. This is the place responsible for turning sound waves into messages that your brain can understand. It's the closest to your brain, so it's also the most protected. Otitis

TOP SECRET:
FOR YOUR EARS ONLY!

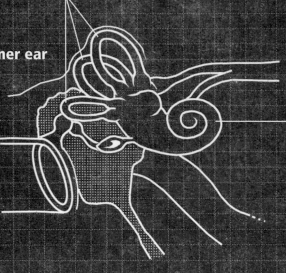

semicircular canals: liquid-filled tubes that regulate balance

(File 4 of 4)
Code name: EAR
Schematic Level 3: inner ear

Parts and Functions:

cochlea: liquid-filled spiral tube that receives vibrations from middle ear, converts vibrations into nerve signals, and transmits them to brain for interpretation as sounds

externa and otitis media don't affect it, beyond interfering with your hearing if the eardrum is under pressure." Otis nodded, but he was looking soggy and weary.

"Let's get you to your bunk," I said. "I'll give you something for your pain and fever, but otherwise I expect your ear will feel better in a day."

"Sir!" the sonar man suddenly called. "Ship spotted at 102 degrees!"

"Ignore it," I ordered. "I'm more concerned with Otis's 102-degree fever."

Otis gasped. "102? My blood will boil!"

"102 degrees Fahrenheit, Otis," I assured him. "That's only 39 degrees in Celsius. Either way, it's higher than it should be."

I turned back to the sonar man. "Dive and order ship-wide silence. The boy needs his rest."

"Aye, Captain," he replied, and Otis slumped gratefully off to his bed.

CARDIOVASCULAR CRISIS
NUT ALLERGY

A renewed optimism had risen in our heroes' hearts. Having escaped the clutches of the fire escape's personnel repellers, our tiring trio had arrived safely outside the second-story landing of the foreboding facility …

D r. Daring tugged with all his strength at the window latch before him. "If we can get through this window, my lab is just inside, at the other end of the hallway,"

Sally peered back down the transparent tube. "No more signs of tear gas," she reported and then staggered slightly. "Whoa! I forgot. I'm a little afraid of heights, and looking down makes me feel dizzy. I feel like my heart is in my throat."

Instantly Dr. Daring was by her side. He put his arm around Sally and pointed past the railing to the car-packed freeway beyond. "Look straight ahead, not down, and the dizziness should pass. Hmm, this reminds me of the last type of reaction in an allergy attack—**cardiovascular**! That's just a fancy term for the system I call the heart highway." Dr. Daring pulled a map from his pocket and spread it before them.

"You can think of your circulatory system as a series of highways. The oxygen carried by your blood is like the cargo carried by delivery trucks on those highways. Your heart is like the central garage where the trucks get their fuel. When you are healthy, the trucks leave the garage fully fuelled—they

DELIVERY TRUCK ROUTE MAP

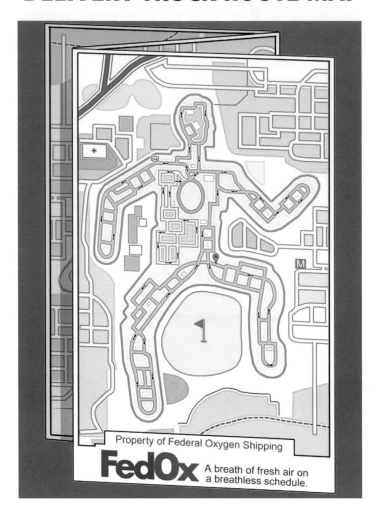

Property of Federal Oxygen Shipping

FedOx A breath of fresh air on a breathless schedule.

Route 1:
Regular Deliveries—
Full fleet, fully fuelled

Route 2:
Wartime Deliveries—
Half fleet, half-fuelled

can drive anywhere on the highways to deliver the oxygen. But during an allergy attack, your body needs that fuel elsewhere for its defenses. The trucks may leave the garage without enough fuel to make all their oxygen deliveries. When muscles or your brain are not getting enough oxygen, you feel weak and light-headed. You may even faint."

Sally, her face pale, was now sharing an edge of the office chair with Billy. "So what can we do to get the trucks fuelled up again?" Billy asked weakly.

"We have to treat the other allergic reactions,"

Dr. Daring replied. "When it's not distracted by responding to an allergen, the heart can go back to doing its job at full strength." He leapt back to the window, took a deep breath, and with a mighty yank wrenched it open.

"The quicker we can treat all those reactions, the better off your body will be. Let's go!" Dr. Daring helped Sally, Billy, and the office chair through the window.

The trio found themselves at the end of a long hallway. At the other end stood a door marked "*Medical Lab.*" But between them and the door stood the foam-soaked skinny scientist, looking angry; the two burly soldiers, looking angrier; and a battered robot eye, looking angriest.

"INTRUDER ALERT!" bleeped the robot, and all the angry eyes turned toward our trio.

"Not again," gulped Dr. Daring.

Have our three heroes finally met their triple match? Will past pursuers perpetrate payback on our protagonists? The answers await you in the action-packed conclusion of "They Came from Mars!"

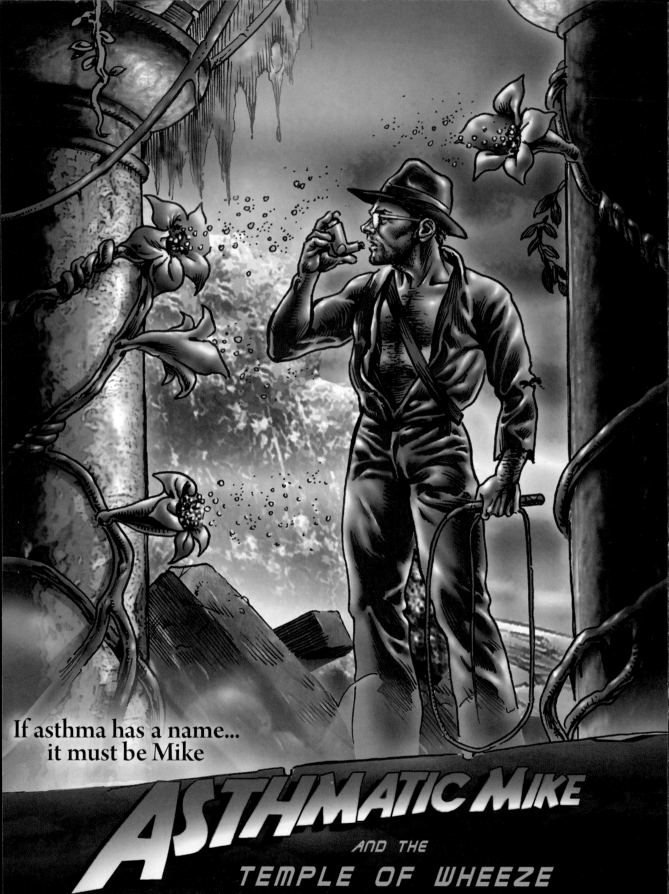

Asthmatic Mike and the Temple of Wheeze
ASTHMA

*H*e had been warned. In the jungle, the humid air hangs as hot and sticky as the lush vegetation. Flowers the size of dinner plates produce enough pollen to make a fish sneeze. Spores yet to be named by science sprout from the decay of fallen trees. Sometimes smoke from simmering volcanoes slips down the mountainside and robs the locals of breath. Yes, he had been warned: the jungle is no place for the weak of lungs. But wherever in the world adventure led, Asthmatic Mike, M.D., would always follow.

He stepped out of the thick growth and crouched beside a stagnant pond. Tipping back his fedora, he produced from his pouch a tattered map. From the trees behind him emerged his companion. Saraniya Rao was a local medical student who knew this jungle the way she knew the layers of the **intercostal muscles**. A fellow adventurer, she had joined Asthmatic Mike on his previous outing, when together they had recovered this map. It revealed the location of the sacred Breath Idol, long thought lost to the world. But it was not lost. It was here in this jungle—waiting for them.

ABANDON ALL BREATH
YE WHO ENTER HERE

"It's there," Mike whispered, nodding first at the map, then at a rock formation at the top of the rise.

"It's here!" cried Saraniya, who had already climbed the hill. Mike sputtered and ran to catch up.

By the time he arrived, Saraniya had already cleared the thick undergrowth from the base of the rocks. Beneath it was a huge stone disk, elaborately carved like a mouth, which had lain hidden for centuries: the gateway to the Temple of Wheeze.

Saraniya was frowning. "Those markings …" Her voice trailed off.

Dr. Mike brushed the last of the dirt away from the intricate inscription in the rock. "'Abandon all breath, ye who enter here,'" he read.

"Asthmatic Mike," Saraniya cautioned, "you can't go in there."

The adventurer removed his hat and wiped the sweat from his brow. "We've been through this before, Sara. With a little preparation, a person with asthma can do anything. People with asthma are movie stars, Olympic athletes—even jungle adventurers." He winked, and his pearly white teeth gleamed in the dappled sunlight. Saraniya rolled her eyes.

Still grinning, Mike pulled a leather-bound diary from his pouch. "And I am prepared. I have been researching the Temple of Wheeze for decades, Sara. I've discovered that the three booby traps inside are based on the effects of asthma. Together we can find ways around them. Let's go!"

The two adventurers grabbed the stone portal and pulled with all their might. The chatter of jungle creatures grew silent as the noise of grinding stone filled the clearing. Centuries-old air rushed out of the opening with a rattling rasp.

Mike replaced his hat with satisfaction. "I have the Wheeze Diary, so I'll go in first—" But Saraniya was already disappearing into the darkness. He scrambled after her.

Mike found her standing in a circular tunnel, squinting against the sunlight from the doorway behind them. He leafed through his diary. "'The breath of the gods,'" he read. "This first tunnel represents a healthy airway."

Saraniya nodded. "The tubes in your body that bring air from your mouth"—she pointed back to the entrance—"to your lungs." Now she pointed forward into the darkness.

Respiratory System

1. **upper respiratory tract**
   - mouth and nose → oxygen enters, carbon dioxide exits

2. **airways**
   - larynx (or voice box)* → vibrates air to create voice
   - trachea (or windpipe)* → main airway
   - bronchial tubes* → airways leading to lungs

3. **lungs**
   - bronchioles* → airways leading to alveoli
   - alveoli* → tiny sacs where oxygen is transferred to blood

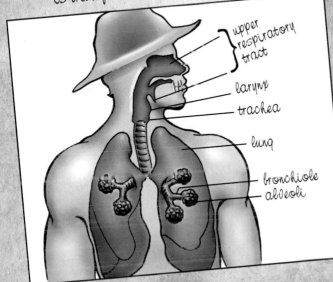

upper respiratory tract

larynx

trachea

lung

bronchiole
alveoli

* see glossary

Healthy Airway

1. thin layer of tissue lining walls
2. normal level of mucus (gross when it comes out of your nose, but an important substance in your body) → protects soft tissue and traps disease-causing germs
3. wide passage for air → easy breathing

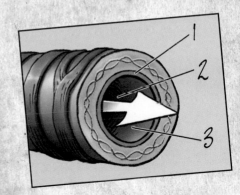

Mike looked around. Hanging cobwebs swayed in a light breeze. First they waved toward the entrance, then they danced back in the direction of the tunnel. "Plenty of room for air to move in and out—a definite sign of easy breathing. Let's go farther."

Soon they were shrouded in darkness. Suddenly there was a thump and Saraniya let out a shriek. "Sara!" cried Mike. The sound of fumbling followed. Then, with a *scritch* and a spark, Mike's torch flared into life. Lit by the dancing flame, Sara sat on the floor rubbing her head.

"Careful," she moaned. "Tunnel's getting tighter." Sure enough, the tunnel had narrowed. Mike moved the torch closer to the wall for a better look.

"Weird," he said, rubbing his eyes. "The flame makes the walls look like they're moving."

"They *are* moving!" yelled Saraniya. Indeed, the walls were expanding toward them.

"Put out that torch!" Saraniya tackled Mike, then shovelled sand on the fallen flame until it winked out.

Seconds later, a blue light sprang to life from Saraniya's keychain flashlight. "I think it's stopped," she whispered.

Mike scowled. "Inflammation."

Saraniya nodded. "When someone has asthma, the lining of the airways is very sensitive—red and swollen."

Mike was checking the diary again. "'An asthmatic airway swells even more if it is irritated by a cold, allergens …'"

"Or smoke from a torch," Saraniya finished. "Maybe you should read ahead in that thing."

"I already have," sighed Mike. "And you're not going to like what comes next."

"Mucus!" cried Saraniya.

"Well done, Sara," Mike replied. "You know your asthma."

"I do, but that's not what I meant." She swung the flashlight beam around to where the tunnel narrowed behind them. A steady stream of viscous fluid was flowing in, and soon they were up to their ankles in the sticky stuff.

"Mucus production is indeed another reaction of asthma," Mike wheezed. "This stuff is present in everyone's airways, but when you're asthmatic like me, you can over-produce it."

"Especially when there is a trigger, like a cold virus, cigarette smoke, a cat, cold air, or even exercise," Saraniya added, stepping gingerly. "The torch is out, so clearly we are the something that's not supposed to be in here. This gross stuff sure makes *me* want to leave!"

Asthmatic Mike struggled to pull his feet out of the sticky liquid. "Actually, in the case of bacteria, mucus is designed to trap it and leave it to die."

"Thanks, that makes me feel better," Saraniya snapped.

"One more booby trap to go," Mike called as he splodged ahead. "**Bronchoconstriction**. It's similar to inflammation in that it narrows the airways. But instead of just the lining swelling, the whole airway tightens."

Beware!
Booby Trap #1

Inflamed Airway

1. thick layer of tissue lining walls
2. grows thicker if agitated by allergens, common cold, smoke, and so on
3. less room for air = asthma attack

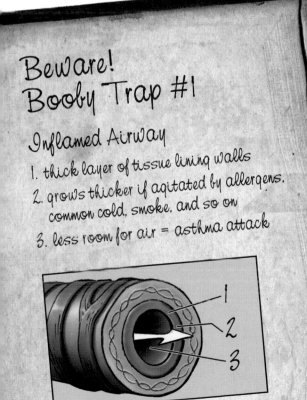

Watch Out!
Booby Trap #2

Excessive Mucus

1. above-normal amounts of mucus in airway
2. grows thicker if agitated by allergens, common cold, smoke, and so on
3. less room for air = asthma attack

"So I noticed," Saraniya grunted as the walls ahead began to collapse inwards. "So what do we do?"

"Asthma attacks can last for minutes or for hours. Shortness of breath, wheezes, and other symptoms can last for days. Best not to wait to see what kind this will be," cried Mike. He grabbed his companion by the arm and together they sloshed down the slimy, shrinking tunnel.

"As I recall," Saraniya said, panting, "there are two strategies for treating asthma: control and rescue."

"Good memory," praised Mike. "Control medications actually treat the inflammation. They take longer to work than rescue medications, but because they treat the basic problem you don't have to use as much rescue medication. It's best to get into the habit of using control medication before entering into areas or activities that might trigger your asthma. A lot of people tend to underuse it and then overuse rescue medication."

"But what if you didn't take any control medication before entering an ancient booby-trapped temple?" Saraniya gasped as she dropped into a crawl. The tunnel was sloping downward now

Heads up!
Booby Trap #3

Bronchoconstriction

1. muscles around bronchial tubes tighten, narrowing airway
2. grow tighter if agitated by allergens, smoke, a cold virus, and so on
3. less room for air = asthma attack

and getting really slippery. "We clearly blew that one. I'd like rescue options, please!"

By now Mike was also scrambling on his hands and knees, but the slope had grown too steep. Down they shot as if on a slimy, stony water-slide. Seconds later they popped out of the tunnel into an open chamber. Saraniya landed on Mike and the tunnel sealed behind them with a *squelch*.

Mike's breath was coming in wet rasps. "Rescue medication," he gasped, "is designed to … relax and open the airways quickly … to allow you to breathe." Fumbling in his pouch, he pulled out a blue plastic canister. "The most common medication … comes in a device … called a puffer … sometimes called an inhaler. Brown puffers hold control medication … and blue ones contain rescue medication."

Quickly he exhaled, wrapped his lips around the mouth of the device, pressed the button, and sucked in. Soon his breathing began to return to normal.

Saraniya looked around. "Hey, your inhaler looks a lot like that thing over there." At the end of the chamber stood an altar of stone. Light streaming from above fell upon a golden object.

"The lost Breath Idol!" Mike whispered. He sprang to his feet and dashed toward the altar.

"Shouldn't you check—" Saraniya began, but Mike had already snatched up the Idol.

Saraniya grimaced as a stone door swung open above them. A dust ball, centuries in the making and the size of a truck, began to roll toward them.

"Dust!" hollered Mike. "A most potent allergen!"

"A dust ball that size will contain billions of **mites**!" Saraniya trembled. "If those tiny creatures get into our lungs, we're goners, asthma or not."

"Back to the tunnel!" Mike commanded, and they sprinted back across the chamber. The dust ball was hot on their heels and picking up speed.

"The tunnel's closed off!" Saraniya warned as they approached the far wall. "Use the Idol!"

Mike swivelled the mouth of the Idol inhaler toward the tiny tunnel opening and pressed its top. A jet of gas whooshed out and the tunnel quickly began to widen.

"The medicine in an inhaler relaxes the muscles that cause bronchoconstriction," Mike explained.

"Come on!" Saraniya pulled Mike into the tunnel just as the rolling dust ball hit. Too large for the opening, it burst into a cloud of particles that sprayed into the tunnel. With a wheeze, the walls began to close again.

"What happens if an inhaler doesn't work?" shrieked Saraniya.

"Inhalers … can be tricky to use," Mike called back, now wheezing again himself. "If you inhale … the wrong way, the medicine … can end up in your throat … instead of in your lungs, where it's needed. A device … called a **spacer** can really help, especially kids. It attaches … to the inhaler and keeps the medicine on deck … and makes sure the medicine gets to where it's supposed to go. See?"

Mike took out his inhaler and connected a spacer tube. Wrapping his lips around the end of the spacer, he activated the inhaler. Saraniya watched the misty medicine gather in the clear tube. Mike waited a moment, then inhaled deeply. The mist disappeared. "See?" he mumbled, his lips still on the spacer.

Saraniya dropped to the ground as the tunnel continued to close. "Use it with the Idol!" she screamed.

"Oh, right." Mike attached the spacer to the Breath Idol and pushed. A sparkling mist gathered in the tube. By now the walls of the tunnel were squeezing at their shoulders. "Ideally, we'd use both a rescue puffer to widen the walls in the short term *and* a control puffer to prevent the airways from closing in the first place. New puffers in different colors combine these, or are longer acting, to keep you breathing easier over the long term."

"*Any* term would be endearing at this point!" groaned his terrified fellow adventurer.

"Just wait," Mike grunted. It seemed the tunnel was about to crush the life out of them, when suddenly there was a great *whooshing* sound. The sparkling mist shot out of the spacer and down the tunnel. Almost at once the whooshing was replaced by a relieved sigh, and the walls once again retreated.

Mike and Saraniya stumbled to their feet and sprinted up the tunnel. They burst out into the sunlit jungle and stood there for a long while, gratefully gulping the fresh air. Finally Mike tipped back his hat and grinned. "I'm glad that worked. When an inhaler fails to work, it's time to go see a doctor or go to the hospital, and I wasn't sure how we were going to get through those tunnels back to the city."

Saraniya gaped at him.

"We can breathe easy now, Sara," Asthmatic Mike said, holding the golden Breath Idol aloft to sparkle in the sun. "Asthma is a condition that should be taken seriously, but with the right training and equipment it needn't keep anyone from having fun. I hope you enjoyed coming along for today's ride."

"Fun? Ride?" Saraniya reached for his neck. "Forget your asthma, *I'm* going to constrict your airways!"

Mike threw back his head and gave a hearty laugh as her fingers closed around his throat. "Oh, Sara! You are my funniest side-kick yet! And what a grip you have. You're stronger than you look. Sara? Sara?!"

ANAPHYLACTIC ATTACK

NUT ALLERGY

Would this be the end of our plucky protagonists? Our heroes had slipped free of scientists, sidestepped soldiers, and even outwitted automatons. But now they had to face all three threats, assembled to blockade our trio's final destination: the medical lab and the treatment that stood between Billy and certain doom …

The scrawny scientist readied his walkie-talkie to call for backup. The steaming soldiers cracked their oversized knuckles. The eerie electronic eye produced, as if from nowhere, metallic arms ending in nasty-looking nozzles.

"The most dangerous allergic reaction," muttered Dr. Daring, "is called **anaphylaxis**."

"What does that mean?" gulped Billy, clinging to the office chair.

"From the Greek," Dr. Daring explained. "*Ana* means 'against' and *phylaxis* means 'defense.' A whole bunch of your self-defenses turn against your own body." The angry antagonists inched closer.

"What does *that* mean?" gulped Sally, also clinging to the wheelie chair.

"It means," whispered Dr. Daring, "that all the reactions we've been talking about can happen at once. Very quickly your body can block all its airways and slow your cardiovascular system until your heart stops."

"That sounds bad," whimpered Billy.

Their tormentors were almost upon them.

"The good news," Dr. Daring said, joining the kids on the chair, "is that just as the attack can start very quickly, it can also be stopped very quickly."

"How?" squeaked Sally as the scientist, soldiers, and sentry bot lunged toward them.

"Take immediate action!" cried Dr. Daring. With a mighty kick against the wall he sent the chair and its passengers shooting down the hall. The scientist scrambled to trap the trio, but he only succeeded in stumbling into the soldiers. The tripped-up troops grabbed for support, taking down the robot in the process.

Our triumphant trio let out a cheer as they rolled to a stop by the door of the medical lab. Dr. Daring swiped his badge through the security lock, and in a flash they were inside, with the door locked behind them.

Sally gawked at the high-tech facility, and especially at the huge window that overlooked the observation hall below, where chaos still reigned.

Quick as lighting, Dr. Daring had Billy on the exam table. He produced an epinephrine auto-injector from a nearby cabinet.

"Hold still now," Dr. Daring advised as he yanked up Billy's pant leg. With the practiced action of a professional, he injected the needle into Billy's thigh.

"**Epinephrine** is a type of hormone called **adrenaline**," explained Dr. Daring as he helped Billy lie back. "It acts like rocket fuel for those oxygen-delivery trucks we talked about. It also tells the drivers to make their most important deliveries first—to the brain and to the muscles that control the airways."

Billy's breathing was already improving. Sally came over and took his hand. "So he's going to be okay?"

"It looks like it," said Dr. Daring, smiling. "But it's important that we get him to a hospital so they can make sure he gets better. The epinephrine

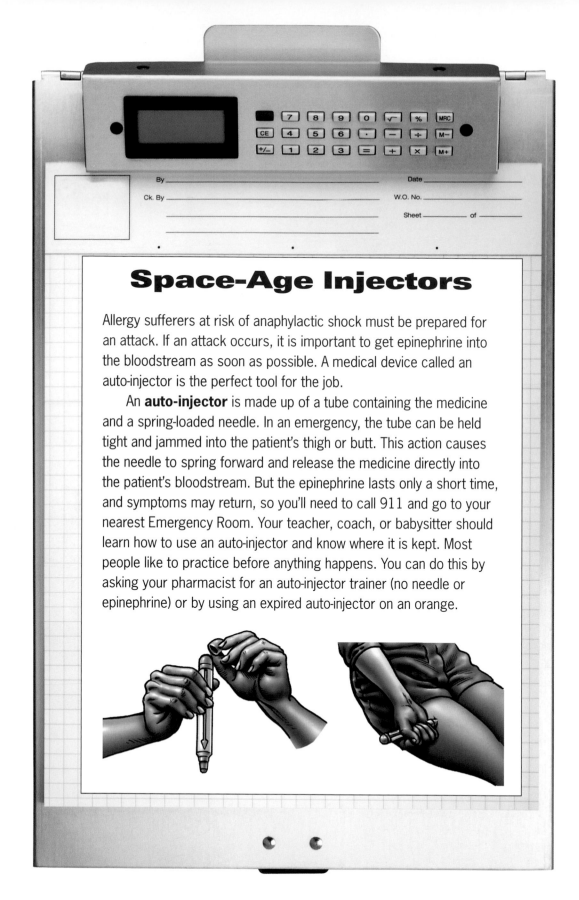

Space-Age Injectors

Allergy sufferers at risk of anaphylactic shock must be prepared for an attack. If an attack occurs, it is important to get epinephrine into the bloodstream as soon as possible. A medical device called an auto-injector is the perfect tool for the job.

An **auto-injector** is made up of a tube containing the medicine and a spring-loaded needle. In an emergency, the tube can be held tight and jammed into the patient's thigh or butt. This action causes the needle to spring forward and release the medicine directly into the patient's bloodstream. But the epinephrine lasts only a short time, and symptoms may return, so you'll need to call 911 and go to your nearest Emergency Room. Your teacher, coach, or babysitter should learn how to use an auto-injector and know where it is kept. Most people like to practice before anything happens. You can do this by asking your pharmacist for an auto-injector trainer (no needle or epinephrine) or by using an expired auto-injector on an orange.

sometimes solves the problem the first time, but it only lasts a little while and patients often need more treatment." He looked down at the observation hall and frowned. "I don't know how easy it will be to get out of here again."

Sally too gazed out the window, and her eagle eyes noticed the telescope. "Leave that to me," she said with a grin.

Sally crawled along the air vent that led from Dr. Daring's lab to a catwalk high above the observation hall. Her head swam when she looked down, so she tried to look to the horizon as Dr. Daring had

suggested. Even so, she knew that, down below, General Patent had managed to arrange his troops in formation. He was barking instructions that involved lots of tanks and missiles. The overhead screen revealed that the arachnid invasion was still going in full force.

Sally took a deep breath, then sprinted along the catwalk until she reached the fat end of the telescope. Standing on tiptoe, she peered into the magnificent magnifier.

"Now they've got a giant girl!" cried the general from below. Sure enough, Sally's face filled the five-story screen.

"No, they haven't," Sally called back. On the screen, her humongous hands could be seen gathering up the army of arachnids. She stepped away from the telescope and leaned over the catwalk railing, displaying her find to the assembled forces below.

"And all you've got are some baby spiders—born on top of your telescope!"

"When did you figure out it was baby spiders, Sally?" asked Dr. Daring as he pumped up the blood pressure cuff on Billy's arm. They were gathered around his hospital bed, and the boy was sitting up and smiling.

"Almost right away," Sally replied, gazing out the window at the now calm city. "But I figured that by the time I'd convinced anybody it might be too late."

"Yeah," sighed Billy. "I guess overreactions can get out of hand pretty quickly, huh, Dr. Daring?"

"They sure can, Billy. They sure can."

We hope your reaction to our stories has been a healthy one. We've sure had a lot of fun explaining these sicknesses in wacky ways to help you understand them. But there is nothing funny about really being sick, and no book is a substitute for visiting a real doctor. If you experience any of the symptoms we've talked about here, or if you have any questions about illnesses of any kind, please talk to your local doctor's office, medical clinic, or hospital. Tell them Dr. Mike sent you.

The End

Further Reading

Macaulay, David. *The Way We Work*. New York, NY: Houghton Mifflin, 2008. (Age Level 9 and up)

Romanek, Trudee, and Cowles, Rose. *Squirt! The Most Interesting Book You'll Ever Read about Blood*. Toronto, ON: Kids Can Press, 2003. (Age Level 9–12)

Walker, Richard. *Ouch! How Your Body Makes It Through a Very Bad Day*. New York, NY: DK Publishing, 2007. (Age Level 10 and up)

Glossary

adrenaline (uh-DRE-nuh-lin)—a hormone that your body makes to give you more energy in times of stress or extra physical effort. What a rush!

allergen (AL-ur-jen)—anything that causes an allergic reaction (see "allergy"). Peanuts, dust, and grass can all be allergens.

allergy (AL-ur-jee)—a condition in which your body reacts negatively to certain materials, such as a particular food, pollen, or dust. These reactions can include watery eyes, a runny nose, a sore throat, itchy skin, an upset stomach, or even trouble breathing (see also "anaphylaxis").

alveoli (al-VEE-oh-lie)—No, not your favorite kind of pasta. Alveoli are tiny sacs that transfer the oxygen you breathe into your lungs over to your blood cells. A single sac is called an alveolus.

anaphylaxis (an-nuh-FILL-ax-iss)—an extreme allergic reaction that causes many symptoms at the same time and very quickly.

antibiotics (an-tee-by-AW-tiks)—medicines that attack bacteria. They don't work against viruses.

antibodies (AN-tee-BOD-eez)—chemicals produced by your body's white blood cells to fight off infections.

antihistamines (an-tee-HIS-tuh-meenz)—medicines that lessen the milder symptoms of an allergic reaction, such as watery eyes, a runny nose, and even itchy skin.

asthma (AZ-muh)—problems with the body's airways that can make breathing difficult. An asthma attack happens when these airways become narrow or blocked by mucus when irritated by things such as allergies, smoke, or exercise.

auditory ossicles (AW-dih-tor-ee AW-sik-ullz)—tiny bones in the middle ear that transmit vibrations from the eardrum to the inner ear. These are the three smallest bones in the human body.

auricle (OR-ick-ull) or **pinna** (PIN-uh)— Listen carefully: the auricle is the part of your ear that sticks out from the side of your head, not the parts that are inside your head.

auto-injector (AW-toe in-JEKT-er) —a spring-loaded needle used for quick delivery of medicine into your body.

bacteria (bak-TEE-ree-uh)— very small and very simple living things that live inside and outside our bodies. Some bacteria are helpful, like the ones in our stomachs that help us take nutrients from the food we eat. Other bacteria can make us sick, such as the streptococci bacteria that cause strep throat.

bacterial culture (bak-TEE-ree-ul CUL-chur)—a crop of bacteria grown on purpose in a lab by doctors or scientists—not the same as the bacteria that grow by accident in your running shoes.

bronchial tubes (BRONG-kee-ul toobz)—the airways in your lungs that connect your trachea (windpipe) to your bronchioles.

bronchioles (BRONG-kee-ohlz)—the smallest airways in your lungs. Bronchioles carry oxygen to your alveoli.

bronchoconstriction (brong-ko-kun-STRIK-shun)—a tightening of the muscles around an airway, resulting in difficulty breathing.

cardiovascular system (kar-dee-oh-VAS-kyoo-lar SIS-tum)— your heart and all the passageways in your body through which blood travels.

cast (kast)—a special bandage that holds broken pieces of bone together while they heal. The bandage is hard on the outside, to keep you from accidentally shifting the bone pieces apart, and soft on the inside so as not to irritate your skin. Available in different colors—signatures sold separately.

cerebrospinal fluid (CSF) (se-REE-bro-SPY-nul FLOO-id) —the liquid layer between your brain and the inside of your skull. It provides extra protection for your brain and allows hormones to travel to your nervous system.

cochlea (KO-klee-uh)—the tiny liquid-filled spiral tube in your inner ear that converts vibrations from the auditory ossicles into nerve signals. Those signals are sent to the brain, which identifies them as sounds. Hear, hear!

comminuted fracture (KOM-in-yoo-ted FRAK-chur)—when a bone is broken in more than two places. Double ouch.

compression fracture (KOM-pre-shun FRAK-chur)—when a bone is broken by being pushed into itself lengthwise.

concussion (kon-KUH-shun)— an injury to the brain caused by a strong impact to the head, which in turn causes the brain to strike the inside of the skull.

diagnosis (dy-ug-NO-sus)—a doctor's identification of an illness based on the patient's symptoms and the results of any medical tests. *Diagnosis* comes from the Greek word for "recognize."

diarrhea (dy-uh-REE-uh)— poop that is very watery.

discharge (DIS-charj)—any unusual liquid-like substance that dribbles out of your body unexpectedly.

ear canal (eer ka-NAL)—the tunnel that leads from your outer ear into your head.

ear wax (eer waks) or **cerumen** (suh-ROO-men)—the sticky yellowish stuff in your ear that prevents dirt and bacteria from traveling farther inside your head. Yes, waxy ears are actually healthier.

eardrum (eer-drum)—a thin, tight membrane in your middle ear that vibrates when hit by sound waves in the air. These vibrations cause the auditory ossicles to move.

epinephrine (ep-uh-NEFF-rin)—another word for adrenaline.

esophagus (uh-SOFF-uh-gus)— the tube through which food travels from your mouth to your stomach.

Eustachian tube (yoo-STAY-shun toob)—a tiny tube that connects your inner ear to your throat and drains mucus away from the middle ear. The Eustachian tube can open and close to control air pressure in the middle ear.

gastric juices (GAS-trik JOOS-es) —the liquids in your stomach that help dissolve food so it can drain into your guts for digestion.

gastrointestinal (GAS-tro-in-TEST-uh-nul) or **digestive system** (dy-JESS-tuv SIS-tum) —your stomach, which breaks down food, and your intestines, which take the nutrients out of that broken-up food and use them as fuel for your body.

germ (jerm)—any microscopic living thing that causes sickness from inside your body.

greenstick fracture (green-stik FRAK-chur)—when a young, soft bone bends and cracks but does not break apart.

histamines (HIS-tuh-meenz)—chemicals released by your body that can fight infection but can also cause the symptoms of an allergy attack. These symptoms can be reduced by taking an antihistamine.

hives (hyvz)—a patchy red rash that can also include itchy bumps. Hives are a common symptom of an allergic reaction.

hormones (HOR-moanz)—chemicals in your body that give instructions to your cells about how to grow and act.

immune system (ih-MYOON SIS-tum)—your body's defense system against disease.

infection (in-FEK-shun)—a condition that occurs when germs get inside your body and multiply in great numbers.

inhaler (in-HAY-lur)—a device that blows a mist of medicine into your airways to reduce the symptoms of asthma.

inner ear (IN-ner eer)—the inside parts of your ear that are closest to your brain: the cochlea and the semicircular canals.

intercostal muscles (in-tur-KOS-tul muss-uls)—the muscles between your ribs that expand and contract to assist with breathing.

large intestine (larj in-TES-tun)—the final tube in the digestive system where nutrients are taken out of digested food. Digested food exits the large intestine as poop.

larynx (LAIR-inks) or **voice box** (VOYS-box)—the muscular organ that causes your vocal cords to vibrate. These vibrations produce sound as air from your lungs passes through your throat.

ligament (LIH-gu-munt)—a flexible strip of tissue that helps to hold bones together at a joint.

lymph node (limf node)—an important part of your immune system, these tiny round bundles of tissue filter out germs. Lymph nodes often swell when they are busy working as filters, so you might feel them in your neck if you have an infection.

middle ear (MID-ul eer)—the parts of your ear between your outer ear and your inner ear. The middle ear includes the eardrum and the auditory ossicles.

mite (myte)—a very tiny insect that feeds on cells that have flaked off other living things, including humans. House dust mites (HDMs) are especially plentiful wherever people live. They are a common allergen and cause of asthma.

mucus (MYOO-kus)—the sticky, slimy stuff found in your nose as well as in your lungs, stomach, and intestines. It may seem gross, but mucus protects your body from germs. Too much mucus in your airways results in an asthma attack.

nerves (nervz)—strands of fiber running throughout your body that carry information between your body parts and your brain.

nervous system (NER-vus SIS-tum)—your body's main communication system. Nerves connect all your body parts to your brain. Information from your brain controls your body's functions, including automatic actions like breathing and planned actions like talking or kicking a ball. Nerves also transmit information to your brain from your body parts, such as pain when you stub your toe or the feeling of soft fur when you pet your dog.

nutrient (NOO-tree-unt)—the fuel that your body extracts from the food you eat. Foods that are good for you provide excellent fuel. Junk food provides lousy fuel.

open fracture (O-pen FRAK-chur) or **compound fracture** (COM-pownd FRAK-chur)—a broken bone that pokes through the skin. Peek-a-boo!

otitis externa (oh-TY-tus ex-TUR-na)—the medical term for swimmer's ear, an infection in the outer part of the ear canal.

otitis media (oh-TY-tus ME-dee-uh)—the medical term for an infection in the middle ear.

otoscope (OH-tuh-skope)—a medical device used by a doctor to look into your ear. An otoscope is made up of a small horizontal cone on top of a vertical handle. Inside the cone are a magnifying lens and a small light. The doctor can also attach a squeezable bulb to the cone for blowing a puff of air into your ear to test the flexibility of your eardrum.

outer ear (OW-tur eer)—the part of your ear that is outside your head (the auricle or pinna) and the ear canal inside that leads to your middle ear.

phalanges (fuh-LAN-jeez)—a fancy word for finger bones.

physical examination (FI-zik-al ex-am-uh-NAY-shun)—a face-to-face visit with a doctor, who inspects your whole body to make sure everything is working. If something cannot be examined properly by looking or touching, the doctor may order one or more medical tests.

pus (puhs)—a white, yellow, green, or brown liquid that results when living tissue fights infection. Pus is made up of white blood cells and dead tissue.

rash—patchy or spotty red marks on your skin that may also be itchy. A rash is a common mild allergic reaction. Hives are a type of rash that also includes bumps.

respiratory system (RES-per-uh-tor-ee SIS-tum)—the parts of your body responsible for breathing, including the mouth, nose, windpipe, lungs, and intercostal muscles.

semicircular canals (SE-mee-SER-kyoo-ler ka-NALS)—liquid-filled tubes in your inner ear. Tiny hairs in the canals sense when the liquid moves and transmit that information to your brain to help you balance.

set (set)—to put broken pieces of bone in place so they can grow back together. Doctors use a cast or a splint to keep broken bones still during the time it takes the bones to heal.

simple fracture (sim-pul FRAK-chur)—when a bone breaks in only one place and the pieces don't cause any serious damage to the nearby muscles, skin, or other tissue.

skull (skul)—the bones that make up your head and face.

sling (sling)—a loop of cloth that hooks around the neck to support an injured arm, like a hammock.

soft palate petechiae (soft PAH-lit pih-TEE-kee-uh)—red spots on the roof of the mouth caused by a bacterial infection such as strep throat.

spacer (SPAY-sur)—a device that makes an inhaler easier to use. The spacer is a tube that attaches to the mouthpiece of the inhaler. When the inhaler is activated, the medicine puffs into the spacer, where it is held until the user is ready to inhale it.

splint (splint)—one or more pieces of hard material fastened around an injured limb to keep a broken bone still.

sprain (sprayn)—the painful swelling that results when your muscles are suddenly pulled the wrong way, such as when you twist your ankle.

strep throat (strep throwt)—a painful sore throat and fever caused by an infection from streptococcus bacteria.

streptococcus (strep-TOE-kaw-kus)—a type of bacteria that causes strep throat. The plural is streptococci.

swab (swawb)—a tissue sample taken by a doctor, who rubs a small cotton-tipped stick on the area he or she wants to test. The sample is often used to try to grow a bacterial culture to confirm a type of infection.

swimmer's ear—See "otitis externa."

symptom (SIMP-tum)—an unpleasant change in your body that signals an illness. Doctors use your symptoms to help identify what kind of illness you have. A sore throat, runny nose, and fever are examples of symptoms.

tendon (TEN-dun)—a tough strip of tissue that connects muscle to bone.

tissue (TI-shoo)—any of the materials that make up a living thing.

tonsillar exudate (TAWN-suh-lur EX-oo-dayt)—pus produced by the tonsils when they are fighting a bacterial infection.

tonsils (TAWN-sills)—small bundles of tissue on each side of the throat. Like lymph nodes, tonsils are part of the immune system and help to fight infection.

trachea (TRAY-kee-a) or **wind-pipe**—the tube through which air travels from your larynx to your bronchial tubes.

virus (VY-rus)—a very small germ that can multiply only by infecting a healthy organism. The more viruses multiply, the sicker you feel. Mild viruses cause minor illnesses like the common cold. Stronger viruses cause more serious illnesses such as chicken pox and measles. Viral infections cannot be fought with antibiotics the way that bacterial infections can.

white blood cells (wite blud selz)—the cells in your body that produce antibodies to fight bacteria and viruses. These mighty immune system warriors surround and attack invaders and also come to the rescue of damaged tissue to prevent that damage from spreading.

X-ray (EKS-ray)—an image of the inside of your body taken by an X-ray machine. X-ray beams pass through your skin and muscle but slow down at your bones, which are denser. Because bone blocks some of those X-rays, it shows up on the X-ray film like a shadow. If a bone is cracked or fractured, more X-rays will make it through the break and show the doctor where that break is. Too many X-rays can make you sick, so X-ray technicians get special training on how to use them safely.

Index